BY JOHN LESLEY

Australian OUTBACK

REDBACK publishing

Redback Publishing
PO Box 357 Frenchs Forest NSW 2086
Australia

www.redbackpublishing.com
orders@redbackpublishing.com

ISBN 978-1-922322-54-8

Author: John Lesley
Editor: Marlene Vaughan
Designer: Redback Publishing

Original illustrations © Redback Publishing 2021
Originated by Redback Publishing

Printed and bound in China

Acknowledgements
Abbreviations: l—left, r—right, b—bottom, t—top, c—centre, m—middle
We would like to thank the following for permission to reproduce photographs: (Images © shutterstock)
Pg9tr katacarix, pg14tl ChameleonsEye, pg14tr Benny Marty, pg14&15 Philip Schubert, pg16 structuresxx, pg19m State Library of Queensland, Australia, pg23tr STRINGER Image, pg24tr State Library of South Australia, pg29bl Edward Haylan

Every effort has been made to contact copyright holders of any material reproduced in this book. Any omissions will be rectified in subsequent printings if notice is given to the publisher.

NATIONAL LIBRARY OF AUSTRALIA
A catalogue record for this book is available from the National Library of Australia

Contents

Where is The Outback?

Australia is a large continent that covers nearly eight million square kilometres of the Earth's surface. In comparison, the UK's area is only about 242,000 square kilometres, and it could fit into Australia thirty-one times.

Australia's twenty-five million people mostly live in its cities and towns. Beyond these is the vast remote area called the Outback.

The Outback is not a place with any definite boundary. When Australians refer to the Outback, they mean the enormous regions of the country that are far away from the sorts of services, transport and facilities that people expect to find in urban areas.

Although the Outback is not a place that anyone can draw exactly on a map, it makes up about 70% of Australia's landmass.

The millions of square kilometres of very remote areas in Australia are home to only a few hundred thousand people.

Other Names?

The regions called the Outback are referred to by other names as well.

THE NEVER NEVER

The term Never Never was made popular by the author Jeannie Gunn in the early 1900s. She was one of the first writers to use the Outback as a location for her stories.

BEYOND THE BLACK STUMP

Whether there ever was just one Black Stump, beyond which there was no European settlement, is unclear. More than one town in Outback Australia claims to be the location of this mythical Black Stump.

BACK-O'-BEYOND

A term that refers to places that are remote and inhospitable to travellers.

What Does the Outback Look Like?

The Outback includes towns, farms, deserts, grasslands, mountain ranges, rivers and even regions along the coast.

FARMING

Cattle and sheep stations occupy large areas in the Outback. Some of these stations have millions of cattle grazing on the land, and they are well over ten thousand square kilometres in size. **This makes them bigger than the island of Cyprus in the Mediterranean Sea!**

TOWNS

Outback towns can be quiet and tiny, or bustling centres for the region. They are always a long way from any other town, and are surrounded by remote regions where few people live.

MINING

Mining occurs throughout the Outback.

WILDERNESS

The Australian Outback contains some of the world's last remaining wilderness areas.

What is an Outback Station?

A station is a cattle or sheep farm in the Outback

Outback Landscapes

Most Australians think of the Outback as a region towards the centre of the continent, away from the coasts and forests. Because there are no boundaries that show where the Outback actually is, different people have their own ideas about whether an area can be called the Outback or not.

The Outback can be hot and dry, or flooded by monsoonal rainfall. Riverbeds that have had no water in them for months, and sometimes even years, can suddenly fill with water that flows from areas hundreds of kilometres away where there has been heavy rain.

THE ANCIENT OUTBACK

Some of the Outback's landscapes are billions of years old. In fact, they are amongst the oldest existing landscapes in the world. The lack of volcanic activity in the Outback over many millions of years has meant that ancient rock formations have not been changed or covered by lava.

A Few Outback Towns

Outback towns vary in size. They range from small Indigenous communities, to the large city of Alice Springs.

ALICE SPRINGS

Alice Springs is a large town located in the Outback. Visitors who want to experience the Outback in a degree of comfort can take day trips from Alice Springs and not have to camp out in the desert.

YULARA

Yulara is the place to go to find out the best way to visit and experience Uluru.

COOBER PEDY

An opal mining town where everyone lives underground to escape the heat.

BIRDSVILLE

The annual horse race in Birdsville turns a small town into a tourist destination.

LIGHTNING RIDGE

An opal mining town.

KATHERINE

The town to use as a starting point to visit the magnificent Katherine Gorge.

MARBLE BAR

One of the hottest places in Australia.

BROKEN HILL

A mining town in far western New South Wales.

The Nullarbor Plain

Although most of the Outback is inland, there is one part of it that reaches all the way to the coast. The Nullarbor Plain is a large and flat limestone plain in the south of Australia. Its edge meets the coast at the Great Australian Bight.

The Nullarbor has little surface water. Any rain that falls seeps underground into the limestone, where there are many caves. The Nullarbor is now far above sea level, but it was formed millions of years ago when it was a seabed.

Deserts in the Outback

Australia has some of the largest deserts in the world. They attracted European explorers, keen to show how the desert could be conquered. Many died while trying.

The Great Victoria Desert is the largest in Australia and one of the biggest in the world. It spans an enormous part of South Australia and also extends into Western Australia.

Australia's wide deserts once isolated the colonial settlements from each other. Sailing around the coast used to be the fastest and easiest way for settlers to travel from one side of Australia to the other, and was the only way colonies on the east and west coasts could stay in touch.

Modern transport options, including travel by air, road or railway, now connect the mainland States of Australia. Travelling through the deserts can still be a risky adventure, even for people who are familiar with the conditions in the Outback.

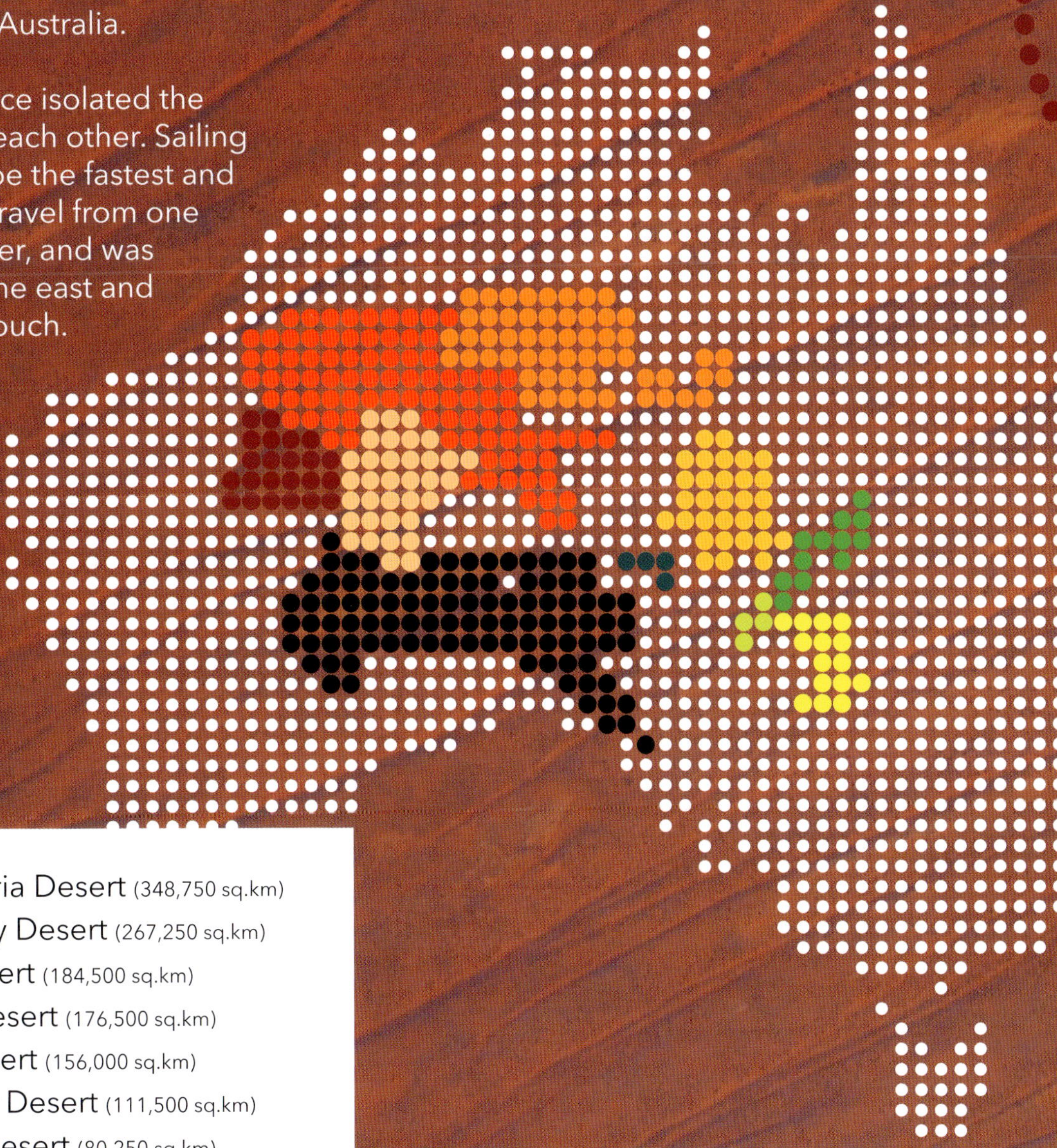

- Great Victoria Desert (348,750 sq.km)
- Great Sandy Desert (267,250 sq.km)
- Tanami Desert (184,500 sq.km)
- Simpson Desert (176,500 sq.km)
- Gibson Desert (156,000 sq.km)
- Little Sandy Desert (111,500 sq.km)
- Strzelecki Desert (80,250 sq.km)
- Sturt Stony Desert (29,750 sq.km)
- Tirari Desert (15,250 sq.km)
- Pedirka Desert (1,250 sq. km)

Kati Thanda-Lake Eyre

Kati Thanda-Lake Eyre is Australia's largest salt lake. It periodically fills with water which then evaporates to leave a salty crust.

As this Outback lake fills, thousands of waterbirds migrate to it from the coast. They include birds such as pelicans and seagulls that are usually only in seaside locations.

Mining the Outback

The red sands and hills of parts of the Outback are a clue to the main ore that is mined there. The red iron ore is a big export commodity for Australia. Mining provides jobs for locals, although many of the mine workers fly in just to do their shifts, and then fly back home to a town or city that is far away from their place of work.

Mining towns in the Outback are sometimes built just for mine workers. When the mines close, the people all leave and the towns become deserted.

Australian Aboriginal People in The Outback

Indigenous Australians have been living in the Outback for thousands of years. Their cultures have an amazingly long history, and are the oldest continuous cultures that exist on our planet.

The desert cultures have produced the art style called dot painting. This traditional art is now admired internationally, with paintings on show in galleries around the world. The Papunya community in the Northern Territory is one of the best-known for its dot paintings.

When the British colonised Australia in 1788, they relied on the legal term *terra nullius*, which means land that nobody owns, to justify claiming ownership of all the land. Today, Indigenous Australians are recognised as the Traditional Owners of large parts of the Outback. Their ownership has been recognised through Native Title legislation.

Many Indigenous communities in the Outback proudly continue to practise their traditional lifestyles, and the Elders are ensuring that younger generations learn the skills and languages of their ancestors.

Australian Aboriginal organisations in the Outback run cattle stations and tourist facilities, and engage in joint operations with mining companies.

Uluru

There is no more famous symbol of the Outback than Uluru. A massive, red rock that rises above the flat desert, Uluru is a sacred site for the local Indigenous people.

The part of Uluru that we can see is only the top of this rock. The rest of it extends for kilometres straight down.

Getting Sick in the Outback

Being so far away from not only hospitals, but even doctors and dentists, means that people living in the Outback have a long way to travel when they get sick.

Outback people have to be resourceful and self-reliant. In the remote Outback, they cannot simply telephone an ambulance to come quickly when they have an injury, so they need to find a way to get themselves to a town where there is medical help.

FLYING DOCTOR

The Royal Flying Doctor Service has been operating across Australia's Outback since the 1920s. Its doctors, nurses and dentists deliver emergency and other health care to people who would otherwise have to endure a long and often dangerous journey by road to find the help they need.

Going to School

In remote areas, children living on stations or in tiny communities do not have any nearby school that they can attend every day. They have to do their schoolwork in other ways.

SCHOOL OF THE AIR

The School of the Air engages with Outback students by using computers to enable teachers and children to interact. Children do their school lessons at home and use the Internet to send their work back to a teacher.

School of the Air class via two way radio, 1960

Before computers existed, the School of the Air used two-way radios to run school lessons. Children and their teachers could not see each other, but they could talk over microphones.

Parents have to spend a lot of time helping their children with lessons when there is no local school they can attend.

REMOTE SCHOOLS

In areas where there are enough children, they attend normal schools. Children may have to travel long distances each day to get to and from classes.

BOARDING SCHOOLS

If there is no secondary school nearby, some parents send their children far away to a boarding school.

IN THE PAST

In the 1800s and early 1900s, before buses and cars were common, some children travelled by horse to school. They would leave their horse in the school yard to graze, and then ride it home in the afternoon. If the family could not spare a horse, the children might be dropped off at school in a horse-driven cart. Having to walk kilometres to school was not unusual.

HOME TUTORS

Some families provide a tutor who lives in the children's home and teaches them their school lessons. When the tutor is a woman, she is often still called a governess, even though this term originated hundreds of years ago. In the past, when there were no Outback schools at all, people who could afford to educate their children employed a governess to teach them at home.

Buying Groceries in the Outback

Although the larger Outback towns have well-stocked supermarkets, people living in remote areas do not have nearby shops that sell everything they need. These residents of the Outback have to make sure they have enough supplies for those times when they may not be able to cross flooded roads to get 'into town'.

HOME DELIVERY OVER A HUNDRED YEARS AGO

The Afghan cameleers used to carry supplies to isolated farms and communities in the Outback. These men had come to Australia in the late 1800s from Middle Eastern countries, including places now in Afghanistan. Along with their famous camels, they crisscrossed the arid areas, selling goods to people who had few other ways of getting their groceries. The Afghans left their little mosques dotted throughout the Outback.

Historic Afghan mosque, Queensland.

Outback Entertainment

People who live in the remote Outback cannot easily go out to see a movie on a Saturday night. If they want to visit an art gallery or go to a favourite sporting event, they may have to travel very long distances, or even spend a few nights away from home.

HORSE RACING

Many areas hold their own local horse races. The Birdsville Races are the most well-known Outback horse races.

RODEOS

Rodeos are popular events where Outback people like to gather for entertainment. The rodeo held every year at Mt Isa is the largest event of its type in Australia. Thousands of people travel there to see the show.

Travelling Across the Outback

ROADS

Roads in the remote outback are often dirt tracks that become mud-traps during the wet season. Four-wheel drive cars are a necessity, and people who are unfamiliar with driving in remote areas need to prepare before setting out on a journey.

DANGERS OF DESERT DRIVING

Places where drivers can buy fuel, food and water may be limited or non-existent, so drivers must take with them everything they will need. If a car breaks down in the Outback, help is not immediately available. In the hot desert, this situation can be life-threatening.

ROAD TRAINS

Road trains are very long trucks, with a number of sections all connected together. People not used to overtaking one of these long road trains in the Outback should take great care. Driving in the Outback is not at all like driving in a city suburb!

CROCODILES

Waterways in the northern Outback are likely to be homes for crocodiles or alligators. A beautiful billabong full of water lilies could be hiding a crocodile just centimetres from the edge.

RAILWAYS

There are two main railways that cross the Outback regions

THE INDIAN PACIFIC

The Trans Australian Railway, also known as the Indian Pacific railway, crosses the Nullarbor Plain. Construction of the tracks started at opposite ends of the continent and met in the middle in 1917.

THE GHAN

The Darwin to Adelaide train, The Ghan, is named after the Afghan cameleers who used their camels to carry the equipment needed to build the railway line. Although construction began in the late 1800s, near Adelaide, the railway did not reach Darwin in the north until the early 2000s.

TRAVEL BY AIR

Outback stations often have their own airstrips, since travel by light aircraft is the only economical way to get in and out of some areas. In the wet season, roads can become impassable. Even after the wet season is over, the damage to roads caused by water flowing over them can make them difficult to use.

EARLY PASTORALISTS

The first European settlers who took their sheep and cattle to the Outback had to walk them all the way. The drovers who undertook these journeys have become immortalised in Australian folklore.

HORSES

Ever since the Outback was first settled, the horse has provided a means of transport, either for riding or harnessed to a cart or wagon. Even today, when graziers use motorcycles to round up livestock, people still ride horses as well.

The Coming of the Telegraph

Landing the telegraph cable, Port Darwin

The settlers who came to Australia were isolated not only from each other across the broad landscape, but also from their friends and families in other countries. Before there was any form of electronic communication, people wrote letters to each other. Carried by slow sailing ships, these letters took months to travel back and forth between Australia and Britain, which was their main destination.

Alice Springs Telegraph Station

All of this changed with the opening of the telegraph line between Darwin on the northern coast and Adelaide in the south. Darwin was connected to a telegraph line which reached to Britain, allowing fast but expensive messages to travel thousands of kilometres overseas. The Overland Telegraph Line opened in 1872. The line ran across the Outback, through mostly desert country. Building it was a major engineering achievement of the era.

Old telegraph machine

Outback Mountain Ranges

Outback Plants and Animals

PERENTIES

SALTBUSH

MALLEE TREES

EUCALYPTUS TREES

CROCODILES

SPINIFEX GRASS

BOTTLE TREES

Water in the Outback

The Outback can be either hot and dry, or flooded with water from monsoonal rains.

Although there is not much water on the surface during the dry season, there is hidden water in the deserts. Underneath large parts of the Outback are massive artesian basins, full of water. Farmers in the Outback access this water by drilling wells and pumping it to the surface.

For many thousands of years, Indigenous people in the dry Outback have relied on the natural springs that allow artesian water to flow to the surface. These springs are rare and sometimes tiny.

Alice Springs, a large Outback town, exists because of the springs that provide artesian water for local use.

Outback Tourism

Government funding to promote the Outback as a fascinating place for tourists has helped to make it more widely known to people outside Australia.

DESERTS

Despite the harsh conditions in the Outback deserts, well-prepared tourists can visit them to experience one of the world's few locations where nature is unspoiled by human interference.

The outback town of Silverton with its Mad Max lookalike vehicles.

OUTBACK TOWNS

Being so remote makes tiny Outback towns both interesting to visit and difficult to get to. Many small businesses in the Outback rely on income from tourism.

What About the Future?

The Outback has existed for millions of years, but what is its future? Will climate change have an impact on it?

MINING

Mining will probably increase as the world begins to need more of the mineral resources that the Outback still has in the ground.

PEOPLE

The human population of the Outback is not likely to increase dramatically due to the lack of water.

FERAL ANIMALS

Feral animals tend to be better at adapting to environmental changes than native animals are. This is what turns feral animals into pests. Climate change could result in an increase in populations of camels, goats and wild pigs, at the expense of the less adaptive native creatures.

Outback Word List

adaptation change in behaviour or body structure that allows an animal to survive

artesian basin underground, natural water stores

cameleer person who looks after camels

cattle station cattle farm

commodities things for sale

drover person who takes livestock across land to another place

evaporate lose water to the air

feral animal a non-native animal that is living in the wild

grazier sheep or cattle farmer

inhospitable not welcoming

lava molten rock that flows out of a volcano

monsoon rainy season

opal gemstone

ore rocks that are mined for their minerals

remote very far away from services

resourceful able to overcome problems

self-reliant able to look after oneself

station cattle or sheep farm in the Outback

telegraph structures that transmit messages along wires

urban referring to a city or town

work shift time a person spends at work

INDEX